2.95

WORSHIP STORIES
Based on Common Objects

WORSHIP STORIES

Based on Common Objects

Walter L. Cook

BAKER BOOK HOUSE
Grand Rapids, Michigan 49506

Unless designated otherwise, all Scripture references are from the Revised
Standard Version of the Bible, copyrighted 1946, 1952 © 1971, 1973.

ISBN: 0-8010-2445-5
Copyright 1980 by
Baker Book House Company
Printed in the United States of America

To
The Young People
of the
First Congregational Church
Millinocket, Maine

Contents

1

Don't Be in a Big Hurry

"And a very large crowd gathered about him, so that he got into a boat and sat in it on the sea; and the whole crowd was beside the sea on the land. And he taught them many things in parables" (Mark 4:1, 2).

Objects: a hoe, rake, spade, and a package of flower or vegetable seeds. The leader may pick up the garden tools and hold them during the talk.

It is fun to have a garden and fun to watch the plants grow. Even if we have only a tiny bit of land in which to sow seeds we can enjoy our garden.

But caring for a garden requires a lot of patience. When we have planted our seeds we have to wait. After the seeds have been in the ground about three days we may be tempted to dig them up to see how they are doing. We want to know, "Have they sprouted?" "Are they ever going to grow?" It seems as though our plants will never come up!

Well, if only we will wait quietly with hope, soon the sprouts will begin to come out of the ground. Then leaves will appear. If we have planted flower seeds we will see buds then blossoms. After a while we will be proud of our garden—even if it doesn't cover a whole acre of land. But in order to have a good garden we have to be patient. We have to wait.

Many things grow slowly (not just flowers and vegetables): our skill at playing some game, our ability to read a story book, knowledge about the world.

Learning about God takes time too. We can't always know in a minute just what he expects of us. Knowledge about him doesn't come all in a rush. If we pray our prayers every day or every night we will get to know how to talk with God.

Jesus wanted his disciples to know about God and how to talk with God. He wanted the kind of followers who would be citizens in the kingdom of God. But the disciples were slow to understand when Jesus tried to teach them. Often he taught them many things in parables. Even then they did not quickly understand his stories. Still he went on loving, teaching, and serving them.

Finally through Jesus' patient teaching they began to know God.

Getting to know God is like watching a garden grow. We can't make peas and carrots and corn grow in a hurry. Some things just don't grow at a gallop—things like gardens and friendship with our Father in heaven.

O God, help us to get to know you—really know you, not only as the creator of the world but as our friend. And if getting to know you takes a lot of time, please give us a lot of patience. In Jesus' name. Amen

2

If You Have a Bad Memory

"Why do you see the speck that is in your brother's eye, but do not notice the log that is in your own eye?" (Matt. 7:3).

Objects: two notebooks, one blank and large, containing many pages; the other small, containing very few pages.

Notebooks are used for many reasons, but mostly they help us to remember. When we want to be sure to remember the name of a new acquaintance, a street address, or a telephone number we say, "I've got to write that down before I forget, because I have a bad memory."

Probably in your home a pad of paper and a pencil are resting right beside your telephone. Some people keep a diary to jot down important things that happen to them. If mother asks us to go to the store for her, quite often she hands us a sheet of paper torn from a notebook on which are listed the articles she wants us to bring back.

Here are two notebooks: one is big and filled with pages; the other is very small and has only a few pages.

Some of us carry notebooks that cannot be seen; they are notebooks of the mind. Some of our minds are like this large notebook; they are filled with unpleasant memories. They contain the mistakes that others have made: unkind words our rivals have spoken about us, thoughtless remarks they dropped that hurt our feelings, selfish things they did, angry glances they cast at us.

Are we people who keep long lists of things that displease us?

Others have minds that are like this tiny notebook; they contain records of our own mistakes. We may feel that we don't have a very long list when it comes to our own failings. Our blunders seem easy to overlook and forget: the time we snubbed a friend, the day we cheated a store clerk, the night we lied about how much we ate.

We would never think of writing down these things. If we did the notebook would be very small.

Jesus had something to say to all of us who keep a record of others mistakes and either forget or make light of our own. He asked people why they saw the speck in the eyes of their neighbors but failed to even notice the log in their own eyes.

The surest way to an unhappy life is to keep adding pages to the big notebook, pages that tell about others who have scowled and growled at us or hurt our feelings.

If we are keeping a notebook at all let us write down the friendly words people speak to us. If we keep that record carefully we will be surprised how large it will grow.

Father, help us to use our memories always in the best way. Amen

3

On Knowing Which Way to Turn

"This day the Lord your God commands you to do these statutes and ordinances; you shall therefore be careful to do them with all your heart and with all your soul" (Deut. 26:16).

Object: any kind of pocket compass that can be passed among the children.

Have you ever been lost? In a big city? In a big building? On a lonely road? Almost all of us, sometime in our lives, have known the really awful feeling of being lost. Perhaps we said, "We don't know where we are." As an example, if we have ever been lost in a forest we may have felt panic coming over us because we did not know what direction to take to get out. We looked this way and that hoping to see something or someone that would tell us how to go so we could get out of the woods, on the road, and back home.

Well, here is a compass that should help anybody who gets lost. It is an instrument to keep us going in the right direction. When you lay it down flat and look at it carefully you can see that the free-moving needle always points north and south and will guide you to walk in a straight line.

A compass *can* be very helpful to us when we get lost in the woods, but too often our minds are so muddled that we do not use it as we should. We may not pay close attention to the pointing needle of the compass. We may not even be sure that the needle is really pointing in the right direction.

As we work and play at home or go to school we need a compass to tell us what is the right way to live. God has given us just such a guide to point us in the right direction.

Long, long ago God spoke to a man named Moses and appointed him leader of people called Israelites. He told Moses many things he should say to the people about laws and commandments. If they followed these rules they would never need to worry about getting lost.

God's commands were a kind of compass that would keep the Israelites going in the right direction in their daily living. His commands and laws can be a guide to us also. They point us in the right direction. They say, "be honest, be truthful, be respectful, be obedient to your mother and father."

Whenever we get that lost feeling and wonder which way to go we can turn to the words of the Bible for help. The Bible is the best compass in the world.

Thank you, God, for caring for us. We need your wisdom and love to guide us in the right way. Every day we are going to try to depend upon your help. In Jesus' name. Amen

4

Love Is Everything
(Valentine's Day)

"If I speak in the tongues of men and of angels, but have not love, I am a noisy gong or a clanging cymbal" (I Cor. 13:1).

Objects: five or six empty cans tied together with a cord in such a way that when they are shaken they jangle and clatter and give out an empty sound. If the cans are new and shiny with bright labels so much the better.

If I held up and shook five full cans of beans, peas, fruit juice, soda pop, or asparagus tips they would make far less noise than these cans on a string. Why do they make so much noise when I shake them?

Yes, it is because they are empty. Of course you know that the noisiest things are not always the most valuable. As you can hear, empty tin cans make a real racket.

In the New Testament we can read the story of a man named Paul who perhaps was the greatest letter writer of all time. After this great Christian had visited a church—and he was doing that all the time—he would write a letter to that church, giving encouragement. And often he would give good advice. At other times he would scold them a little for their faults.

One of Paul's letters contains a passage that is a great favorite among many Christians. It is called the "love chapter," and begins this way: "If I speak in the tongues of men and of angels, but have not love, I am a noisy gong or a clanging cymbal." This is a good chapter to read on this Sunday before St. Valentine's Day when we will be writing "love" on all the paper hearts we make at school.

In the love chapter Paul says that if we do all the good in the world but do not have love and good will in our hearts then the good things we do are only empty deeds.

Suppose we take all the dimes in our piggy bank (if we have one) and put them in a church envelope to help feed hungry people. If we are proud of our good deed but have no sincere love in our hearts for people who are starving, then we are like noisy gongs and clanging cymbals—or like empty tin cans.

If we have studied the lesson for our church school class and can repeat loudly many Bible verses we may feel a little proud of ourselves. But unless we love God and his Word and treat others with good will we are like empty tin cans.

When all day we have been obedient to mother and father, running errands for them, and helping them all we can, we may feel satisfied with ourselves. Be sure that what we do for them is always in love. Love is everything.

Every day, God, may we be kind and thoughtful of others. May our good deeds be done in quietness and always in love. In the name of Jesus. Amen

5

If You Can Make Only One Gift

"But Jesus said, 'Let her alone; why do you trouble her? She has done a beautiful thing to me' " (Mark 14:6).

Object: one roller skate.

Back and forth. Back and forth. A girl on roller skates was having fun on the sidewalk. She was a skillful skater: sometimes she would skate fast, make quick turns and then come back again. After awhile she was joined by another girl who wasn't a clever skater at all. The new girl was clumsy. She bumped up and down, could not make quick turns, and was a much slower skater. Can you guess why the second girl was not a good skater?

Yes, she had only one skate. But she had a lot of fun on that one skate. You might say to her, "Hey, Sally [or whatever her name], you ought to have two skates." And maybe she would say, "I sure enough know that, but I've only got one skate. I'm going to have as much fun as I can on my one skate."

Sally, probably a girl in about the third grade, would be a lot wiser than some of us who have been out of the third grade for twenty or more years.

She made the most of what she had and didn't whine about

what she didn't have. It is important when we make a gift to Jesus that we give what we have and not complain because we don't have more to give him. How wonderful it would be if we had many rich presents to give him! But if we do have just one and we give it gladly we need not be ashamed.

Perhaps you remember a story in the Gospel of Mark about a woman who made a wonderful gift to Jesus. She entered a room where he was eating a meal with some friends, went up to him carrying a jar of sweet smelling ointment, broke the jar, and poured the perfume on his head. It was a very costly present to him and it was her way of showing her appreciation for her friend Jesus. Some people saw her make the gift to Jesus and said she should have sold the ointment, taken the money she got for the sale, and given it to the poor. Jesus defended her kind act and said, "Let her alone; why do you trouble her? She has done a beautiful thing to me."

The woman gave to Jesus what she could; we too are to give him what we can. Maybe we can make only one gift to him—and that gift may not seem like a big one. We really would like to do so much more. But just as Sally on one skate was having a wonderful time, so may we be joyful when we make our gift to Jesus.

Thank you, God, for all you have done for us. Your gifts to us seem so great and important. Help us when we have a present for you to give it joyfully. In Jesus' name. Amen

6

The Palm Sunday Parade
(Palm Sunday)

"And they brought it [the colt] to Jesus, and throwing their garments on the colt they set Jesus upon it. And as he rode along, they spread garments on the road" (Luke 19:35, 36).

Objects: a heavy, hooded winter jacket, a rain coat and hat, a costume to wear at a party, a pair of camp shorts, and a pair of pajamas. The pieces of clothing may be placed on a stand or table before the service; during the presentation several children may be chosen to hold up the different articles of clothing.

There are many kinds of clothes to wear: clothes to wear in winter, when it rains, when we go to a party, when we go to camp, when we go to school, and when we go to bed.

When you get a new jacket or a new pair of jeans, or a new sweater you are probably proud of them and you may hope that some of your friends will notice your new things and praise them. I guess everybody likes to wear new clothes.

Although we should be pleased when our parents buy us something new to wear we should not come to care *too* much about how our clothes look. If we are too proud of fine clothes we may be tempted to hold back from having fun on the school playground because we are afraid of getting dirt on our shoes or jacket. (After awhile we won't care so much.)

People on the first Palm Sunday must have liked pretty clothes as much as we do, but they took off some of them and put them in the path of the donkey on which Jesus rode when he entered Jerusalem. Do you remember the story about how all the people were so glad to welcome Jesus into the city that they cried out: "Blessed be the King who comes in the name of the Lord! Peace in heaven and glory in the highest"?

Jesus' disciples and friends found palm branches and spread them on the highway. But the most astonishing thing they did was to take off some of their coats and outer garments and place them on the road in front of Jesus as he rode.

Can you imagine girls and boys like yourselves putting jackets and sweaters on the road so that Jesus' donkey could walk over them? Well, the people were so happy about Jesus that they forgot all about how much they liked their clothes.

This thing the joyful people did shows how great they believed him to be. What they were showing was this: nothing is too good for Jesus the King, the Son of God.

Thank you, God, for the story of the first Palm Sunday. We wish we could have been there to see the big parade. Help us to honor Jesus this day and every day just as his followers did so long ago. Amen

7

The Most Wonderful Sunday of All (Easter)

"When he was at table with them, he took bread and blessed, and broke it, and gave to them. And their eyes were opened and they recognized him . . . " (Luke 24:30, 31).

Object: a loaf of bread. At the appropriate moment during the telling of the story, the loaf may be broken by the worship leader.

Suppose some morning you look down the road from your house and see a girl coming toward you who looks like a friend or a schoolmate. She's quite a distance away so you're not sure just who she is.

Well, when she gets a little nearer you notice the jacket she is wearing and you know right away who she is even when you can't see her face clearly at all.

We discover who people are in different ways, not only by the jackets and caps they wear but often by the sound of their voices or the way they walk and run.

Once hundreds of years ago, just a few days after Jesus was crucified on a cross, two of his friends were taking a long walk.

They were sad because Jesus had been killed, and they were telling each other how good a friend he had been to them. All at once as they walked they were joined by a stranger who took part in their conversation. He was their friend Jesus, but they did not recognize him.

After they had walked a long way they came to the place where the two men planned to stay all night. Because the sun was setting and darkness was coming on they said to the stranger, "Stay with us." So Jesus went in to stay with them. And still they did not know who he was.

After awhile all three sat down to supper and when they did that he did something that made them recognize him. As he sat at the table he took bread, thanked God for it, and broke it. Immediately they knew who he was, and they were filled with happiness. That same night they walked the long distance back to the city of Jerusalem to tell the other friends of Jesus that he was alive.

Today is Easter, one of the happiest Sundays of the whole year. In a way it is a more joyous day than Christmas. We are happy on this day especially, because we remember that Jesus rose from the dead and is alive.

Each time communion takes place in this church we remember how, long ago, Jesus made known his victory over death by breaking a loaf of bread with his friends.

Thank you for this happy day, God. We praise you for raising your son Jesus from the dead. We want to walk with him all our lives. In his name. Amen

8

Putting Color into a Day

"And the next day he took out two denarii and gave them to the innkeeper, saying, 'Take care of him; and whatever more you spend, I will repay you when I come back'" (Luke 10:35).

Objects: two large glasses of water and a dropper containing bright red fluid.

Here are two glasses of water. I am putting one drop of red coloring into one of the glasses. You can watch the red coloring move down into the water. But the water doesn't get very red. One drop of red does not make much difference in the color of the water.

In the other glass of water I am dropping twelve drops of red coloring. Now see the difference: the water in this second glass is bright red.

This experiment might make us think of the way we often do kind things for others. Some of us pass out our good deeds one at a time, or we could say one *drop* at a time.

Let us say that some friends or acquaintances need our help. Instead of helping them warm-heartedly and generously we may feel that we only want to do one thing for them—which doesn't help very much. It is not that we intend to be stingy or

21

mean or miserly, our trouble is we think that one good act is all anyone should expect of us. "There," we may say, "that's my good deed for the day." Then we feel we have done our duty.

Maybe we could have done a dozen good things for a friend who was in trouble. God calls us to be truly generous with all who need our help.

Can any of you tell what is one of Jesus' best known stories? If you should say "the parable of the good Samaritan" you would be right. That Samaritan was really a generous giver. Remember how one day he found, in a ditch beside a road, a man who had been beaten and robbed and left half dead. When the Samaritan came by he picked up the wounded man, bandaged his wounds, put him on his own donkey, and carried him to an inn. He did all he could for the injured man. Then instead of saying to himself, "There, I've done my good deed for the year," he gave money to the innkeeper and asked him to care for the wounded man. After that the Samaritan promised to return with more payments. He was a most generous giver.

Perhaps before you go to bed tonight you will meet someone who needs your help—someone who is lonely and needs a friend, or is gloomy and needs a cheering word, or is handicapped and needs encouragement.

Give generously of your help to such a person, not just a drop or two of kindness.

God, may I give to others as though I have all the riches in the world and want to share them. In Jesus' name. Amen

9

You Have a Powerful Partner (Thanksgiving)

"Jesus then took the loaves, and when he had given thanks he distributed them to those who were seated; so also the fish, as much as they wanted" (John 6:11).

Objects: a candle in a small holder and an electric cord with a 100-watt bulb at its end. The cord should be plugged in so that when a switch is snapped the bulb will light.

In your home you always have a partner who will go to work for you. It is always waiting to serve you. All you have to do is push a button and that partner will light up your room. It brings voices to you through your radio. It runs your record player and TV. It roasts your turkey or chicken for Thanksgiving. It is waiting to go to work for you.

Of course you know the name of your partner is electricity, and it gives you and me all the light we need.

This candle doesn't give much light. It helps a little, but when we want to read a book at night, or write a letter, we need all the light we can get, and that's when we are thankful for electricity. See how much light we get from this bulb!

Do you ever stop to think how grateful we should be that scientists discovered how to use electricity? Probably we don't think about it very often; we just take for granted all our powerful partner does for us.

We take many other things for granted, too: a house to protect us from storms, cereal for breakfast, socks and sneakers, shirts and jeans, a few books to read, and people who love and care for us.

At Thanksgiving time let us be grateful for our electricity partner and for many other advantages that help us in our daily living.

When Jesus was on earth he did not have electricity as a helper, nor many of the conveniences that we enjoy today. But he did have much for which to be grateful. Once out in the wilderness he gave thanks to God for just fish and bread. He took this food and fed a crowd, but before he fed the people he gave thanks to his Father in heaven.

Do we thank God each day for all we have? If we had to read a book or write a letter by candlelight would we not then be grateful if someone pressed a button and flooded the room with light? On Thanksgiving Day let us be sure to thank God not only for our electricity partner but also for many other blessings.

God, we enjoy so many good things! We can't begin to count them. But even if we can't remember them all, please give us thankful hearts. In Jesus' name. Amen

10

A Whole Concert on One String

"But he who had received the one talent went and dug in the ground and hid his master's money" (Matt. 25:18).

"Then you ought to have invested my money . . . , and at my coming I should have received what was my own with interest" (Matt. 25:27).

Object: a musical instrument—a violin, banjo, ukulele, mandolin, or guitar—with all strings removed but one.

Once years ago a famous violinist walked onto the stage of a concert hall. As he began to play before a large audience the strings on his violin began to break. One after another they snapped until only one remained. That one string did not break, and the great musician played all his selections on a single string.

Perhaps the violinist inwardly said thank you to God that one string remained strong and useful.

Some of us may think that we are a little like the violinist—at least in one way. He had but one string on which to play music. We may feel we have only one skill, one ability, one talent to work with. If that is what we think about ourselves we may be in danger of doing nothing.

Let us decide that our one skill is important; let's put it to good use.

Jesus once told a story about a man who, when he was going on a long journey, put three of his servants in charge of his property. He gave to one about $5,000, to another $2,000, and to a third man $1,000. The first two men used the money they got to make more money. But the man with the smallest sum, feeling himself unimportant, was afraid to put the money to work. Instead he dug a hole in the ground and hid the $1,000. He did not make the most of the money. When the owner returned he asked the servants how they had used the sums he had left with them. The men with the larger amounts were rewarded for the gains they had made. But the man with the smallest amount was scolded because he did not put his share to work.

If you and I have only one small talent are we using it? Are we thinking how we may put that talent to work for God?

Perhaps we make friends easily. That may not seem like a useful talent, but it really is. Sometimes a lot of skill is needed to become a friend to a bashful or quiet person.

Do we play a musical instrument of some kind? Maybe we could play one or two pieces for people who are old and shut-in and would enjoy a little company as well as our tunes.

If we have only one talent we must not be discouraged, but put it to work.

God, we know you want us to be useful. Help us to work for you and people everywhere in the world who may be in trouble or in need. In the name of Jesus. Amen

11

Can You Remember What You Look Like?

"For if anyone is a hearer of the word and not a doer, he is like a man who observes his natural face in a mirror; for he observes himself and goes away and at once forgets what he was like" (James 1:23, 24).

Object: a fairly large mirror which may be held in front of each child for a moment.

I wish that instead of the mirror I am showing you now I could have found one used by girls and boys about the time the New Testament was written. In those days mirrors were made of polished silver or brass; they were small and could be held in your hand.

For just a moment I'm going to hold this looking glass in front of you so you can see yourself. Now you know what you look like. I suppose you have seen yourself many times before when you were asked to comb your hair as you were getting ready for school. Probably you don't spend much time looking into mirrors; perhaps when you do you don't like what you see!

A certain boy I know is, as we say, pretty good looking. But he doesn't like to look in a mirror because he says his ears stick out.

A fourth-grade girl I know, doesn't like her mirror because when she glances into it she sees about thirty freckles gathered all around her nose, like a cluster of stars around the moon.

In the New Testament is a letter by a man who describes himself as "James, a servant of God and of the Lord Jesus Christ." Some people have thought this letter writer was a brother to Jesus. Anyhow, he was a follower of Jesus. In the letter James tells about a man who looked in a mirror, saw his face for a minute, then went on his way, forgetting all about how he looked. That man was like some of us who come to church to worship God. We listen to the Bible readings, the prayers, and the minister's sermon, then go off down the street forgetting everything that was said.

Coming to church and listening to the Word of God in the Bible should make a big difference in the way we live and act after church.

In church we hear that we should help to feed the hungry, give clothing to those who are cold, and visit those who are in prison. To forget what we have heard as soon as the service is ended is like glancing into a looking glass and then forgetting right away what we look like.

O God, even if we forget how we look in a mirror, never let us forget people who may need our help. In the name of Jesus. Amen

12

Do You Have a Good Memory?

"And it shall be to you a tassel to look upon and remember all the commandments of the Lord, to do them" (Num. 15:39).

Object: any kind of tassel, a small hanging ornamental bunch of threads, small cords, or strands hanging on a knob or button. The brighter the color the better. Also objects such as a piece of bright string and a colored notepad may be used in the presentation.

Do you have a good memory? When mother and father ask us at breakfast to do an errand after school do we remember to do it? When the teacher at school asks us to bring our lunch money next day do we remember to bring it? When we make promises to our friends do we remember to keep them?

Do you know any special ways you can help yourself remember the things you ought to do?

The people of Israel had an unusual way of reminding themselves of the words of God. They were told by Moses to attach tassels to their clothes so that all the time they would keep in mind their duty to God. Each time they looked down and noticed the tassel they would think of God's commandments and do them.

Some people today wear a cross of wood or of gold as a reminder of how Jesus suffered and died for them. Others hang pictures of Bible scenes in their living rooms and in their dens so they will not forget that they are the children of God and must honor his words.

Perhaps you have heard of someone who ties a piece of string on his finger so he will remember to do something that needs to be done. Some people use a pad of paper to jot down errands they must run. Others keep an engagement book to help them remember their appointments. And of course mother and father write out a grocery shopping list to use when they go to the market.

All of us need reminders to jog our memories. A big question is, how can we remember to do right and obey God? Perhaps the best reminder is not a tassel, or a piece of string around your finger, or even a bright colored notepad, but to think often about the words of Jesus we find in the New Testament. If we think of these we will remember what he wants us to do.

O God, when you speak to us in our hearts help us to listen to every word. And once we know the things you expect of us may we never forget them. In the name of Jesus. Amen

13

Take a Look Inside

" . . . this people honors me with their lips, but their heart is far from me" (Mark 7:6).

Objects: three boxes of different size and shape. The exteriors of the boxes should be attractive, or in some way appealing, as though they contained gifts.

I have a surprise for you today, although you may not think it is a good surprise at all. Here are three boxes on the table and I suppose you are wondering what can be in them. Every time the parcel post service brings a package to your house probably the first thing you say is, "I wonder what's in that box."

Well, let's see what is in these boxes. Box one is empty. Box two is surely a pretty one, but it's empty also. Now box three is smallest of all, but often times small packages contain great treasures. Do you suppose this box has something valuable in it? No, this is just like the others—empty.

Jesus had something to say, not about empty boxes, but about empty hearts. He said it to some enemies who were criticizing his disciples. These enemies were called Pharisees and it seems, when we read about them in the Bible, that they were always following him and his friends to bother and pester.

One day these Pharisees criticized Jesus' disciples for not keeping the religious rules of the Jews. Right away Jesus told them that their hearts were far from God. He said they often did *say* the right things but were not *doing* the right things. So their words of praise to God were like these boxes: empty.

When we come to church we honor God by standing and singing praise to him. When we bow our heads and thank him for all he does for us we are honoring him. When we join in the responsive reading we are doing the same thing—we are honoring God with our lips. These things are what we do in church and they are right to do.

Let us be sure that we honor God not only with our lips but also honor him in our hearts. When we obey his voice and do the things he wants us to do then we are reverencing God.

God does speak to us, you know. Every once in awhile we hear his voice inside us that tells us to do what we know is right. When we obey that voice and do what is right, then the words of praise we speak and sing in church will not be words that are empty.

O God, help us to be sincere when we sing songs of praise to you. May the good words we speak and sing be always backed up by the good things we do. For Jesus' sake. Amen

14

What Have You Been Doing?

*"Now when they saw the boldness of Peter and John... ,
they recognized that they had been with Jesus" (Acts 4:13).*

Object: a house painter's white cap showing prominent green, yellow, blue, or orange daubs of paint. The leader might put on the cap for a moment during the presentation.

If I should ask you, "What do you suppose I have been doing lately?" you would probably say, "By the looks of your cap you have been painting your house or something." My cap has green spots on it; so you may decide I have been giving my house a coat of green paint. If my cap had orange spots on it you might say that something in my house has been getting a coat of orange paint.

If we run into our house at dinner time with a black eye mother may think we have been in a big fight or that we have been hit by a softball bat.

When our feet get soaking wet mother will know that we've been wading in a puddle or running through wet grass.

If we come home from school with a poor report card mother and father may decide we have been fooling around in our math, science, and reading classes.

Many hundreds of years ago two men named Peter and John did really wonderful things. They healed diseases and cast devils out of people. They were also forceful speakers. People who were watching them were astonished that Peter and John had such powers. They asked, "How can these two men do and say such marvelous things?"

Finally someone came up with the answer. The two men were able to perform wonders because they had been close friends with Jesus. They spent hours and days in his company.

Peter and John went everywhere with Jesus. They watched him heal people of their diseases. They listened to his teachings and saw his great courage. They observed how he loved all people who were in trouble and needed help. People recognized that Peter and John had been with Jesus because he left his mark of influence upon them.

Today, every person who has been with Jesus and has accepted him as friend and guide and Savior will be sure to show it. When we stay close to him, doing the things he wants us to do, then our sisters and brothers and schoolmates and neighbors will know that, like Peter and John, we have been with Jesus. We will show it by our goodwill and kindness to others. People will know what we have been doing.

Help us, God, to walk and talk with Jesus every day. May some of his kindness and greatness become a part of us. In his name we pray. Amen

15

The Way We Write Our Names

"At that time Herod the tetrarch heard about the fame of Jesus" (Matt. 14:1).

Objects: a piece of chalk, a pencil, a ballpoint pen, and a large sheet of drawing paper.

At school we write with chalk, pencils, and sometimes with a ballpoint pen. Probably we have three or four pencils in our desk at school. We could not learn very much in our room at school if we did not use pencils.

Writing our names is one of the first ways we put our pencils and pens to work. We learn to write our names on paper. Sometimes we print our initials on fences, on sidewalks, on rocks, and even on the sides of houses. This may get us into big trouble.

When we give our spelling papers to the teacher we use a pencil to write our name on them so she will know where they came from. But after awhile we may not need to write our names on the papers we pass in. The teacher knows by the quality of work, by the neatness of the paper, and by how many times we had to erase, just who did the paper. These signs tell her who we are as plainly as though we signed our name.

The first verse of Matthew 14 contains the phrase: "the fame of Jesus." Jesus went all about his country doing wonderful and kind things for men and women, boys and girls. He became famous for giving blind people their sight, for healing the deaf, the lame, and even lepers.

Everywhere Jesus went he wrote his name in kindness and helpfulness upon the lives of troubled people. Of course he did not use a pencil or pen to sign his name on his deeds, but his hundreds of kind acts were his signature for everyone to read. That was how Herod the king heard about the fame of Jesus.

How are *we* known among our acquaintances and friends?

If we are generous with others we will be known and thought of as free-hearted and thoughtful. If we are stingy and always trying to get everything for ourselves we'll be known as selfish people. We will not need to sign our names on our deeds; we will be known by the deeds themselves.

If we do not hold grudges against others we may become known as boys and girls who are ready to forgive.

If we often take time to speak with another girl or boy who always seem to be alone we'll be known as friendly people ourselves.

O God, we wonder whether so far today we have been thoughtful and kind. Have we been stingy or unforgiving or have we spoken unkindly of anyone? If we have been mean at all to anyone, forgive us. We would like to be known as people who care for others. In Jesus' name. Amen

16

Treasure Old and New

"Therefore every scribe who has been trained for the kingdom of heaven is like a householder who brings out of his treasure what is new and what is old" (Matt. 13:52).

Objects: a basket or small chest containing a much used pocket notebook, scissors, a warm cap, a can opener, a bright scarf or necktie, two new red pencils—unsharpened, a bar of soap still wrapped.

In this basket are some old things and some new things. On the right side of the table I will put the old things; on the left side I will put the new. I suppose you might say that these are all treasures because some of them have been used by our family or are going to be used or worn.

Some of the new things you see here are as valuable to us as the old.

In one of his stories Jesus tells about a man who owned a house that was filled with treasures. We can only guess what kind of treasures he owned. Perhaps he had a collection of gold coins hundreds of years old, or maybe a pearl necklace that belonged once to his great, great grandmother, or a battered old book filled with ancient wisdom.

Neither can we know what were his new treasures. Perhaps he had recently brought home from a store a colorful new coat, or a handsome diamond ring. At any rate he had what we call a treasure trove. And from it he could bring out many valuable things, both new and old.

Of course we all like new things: new sweaters, new books, new games, new friends. But the old can be just as useful as the new. Sometimes we hang onto the old and pass up the new. Both can be to us a kind of treasure.

On the street near your home may live a girl or boy you have known for three or four years or even longer. You play together and walk to school or ride the bus together. You are friends—old friends. Far down at the end of your street is another girl or boy who is in your grade at school. He or she is already becoming your friend, a new friend. Both old and new friends can be your valued treasures.

Perhaps you have heard some beautiful Bible stories (like the one about Jesus in the temple when he was twelve years old). These old familiar stories are like riches to you. But perhaps you have found some other stories, in the Old Testament, that are intensely exciting. Both old and new stories can be lively and inspiring.

It is wonderful to select things from a treasure box whether they are old or new.

Thank you, God, for all the good things that come our way. Help us to enjoy them and be thankful for them. In the name of Christ. Amen

17

Build Your House Upon a Rock

"Every one then who hears these words of mine and does them will be like a wise man who built his house upon the rock" (Matt. 7:24).

Objects: a solid looking rock and a container of sand. During the presentation the sand might be poured onto a table to display its lack of firmness.

Perhaps one day on your way to school you picked up a stone, held it in your hands for a minute, then gave it a throw (I hope not at a window or at an electric light).

Stones or rocks are so common that we pay little attention to them. But rocks are of great value to us. We could not live without them. Soil in which we grow flowers and vegetables is made up of crumbled rocks and bits of dead plants. Much of our air and water come out of rocks. Without stones or rocks there would be no grain, no animals, no people.

Every day we depend upon rocks. Bridges are made of stones, and maybe the driveway to your garage is, too. Even the glass in our windows comes from rock.

It may seem strange, but all of us are living right now on a huge ball of rock.

Jesus once talked with his friends about a rock foundation. He told about a wise man who built his home upon a rock. After it was built there came a mighty wind that beat upon the house. Heavy rain fell upon it, even floods swirled around it, but it stood firm against the wind and floods because it was built upon a rock.

Another man built his house upon sand and saw *his* house washed away when the wind and rain hit it hard. He should have given the house a foundation of rock.

After Jesus told his story about the two builders he said that those who obey his words will be like the man who built his house upon a rock.

Perhaps you remember a lot of the words Jesus spoke that will be a help to us no matter what happens. Some of those words may seem hard for us to obey, but they are the rock foundation on which we must build our Christian life.

Jesus urged his friends to build lives upon sincere prayer, fair judgments of others, forgiveness of those who do us wrong, kindness to all who are in need, and honesty about our own mistakes and short-comings.

The commands he gave to his friends so long ago are the same ones he gives to us.

Thank you, God, for the words of Jesus and for his story about the two men who built houses. Help us to build our own Christian lives on his words. In his name. Amen

18

When Things Get All Tangled Up

"And he withdrew from them about a stone's throw, and knelt down and prayed, 'Father, if thou art willing, remove this cup from me; nevertheless not my will, but thine, be done'" (Luke 22:41, 42).

Object: any kind of a fishing line badly tangled.

A boy was sitting on the back porch of his home trying to straighten out a snarled fishing line. It was a mess and looked like this.

The boy worked and worked to untangle the line because he wanted to go fishing. But the harder he worked the worse the tangle became.

The boy's father came out on the porch and watched for a minute while the boy fussed with the line. Finally the father said, "Son, if you want me to I'll try to unravel that line for you." After awhile the father got it all back on the reel and ready for the boy to go fishing.

Once in awhile we get all tangled up ourselves. We get up in the morning and right away everything begins to go wrong. At breakfast we dump cereal into our lap or spill fruit juice on the table, which makes mother and father disgusted with us. We go to school and the teacher gets cross with us because we don't settle down to work as quickly as we should. On the way home from school we have a disagreement with our best friend who says, "I'll never speak to you again." At supper dad says the family car is broken down and is being repaired at the garage, so our Saturday picnic is called off.

We go to bed at night feeling that life is all a snarled up mess.

Well, God can help us when life gets into a snarl. He may not make everything right just the way we want. (Our days will always have a few kinks in them.) But God is ready to help us if we go to him in prayer and put our troubles and problems into his hands.

Jesus' days were filled with trouble—yet he was often a joyous person. What did he do with trouble? Think of him in the Garden of Gethsemane when he knew that soon he would be arrested and crucified. (Trouble? We don't have any idea what real trouble is!) He put his problems and his life in his Father's hands. Just before his enemies killed him he asked his Father for help. He prayed, "Father, if thou art willing, remove this cup from me; nevertheless not my will, but thine, be done." God gave him strength to bear suffering and agony.

We do not suffer the way Jesus did. But we do have difficulties, disappointments, and discouragements. They should be put into the hands of God. We can trust him; he will always be with us, just as he was with Jesus in the Garden of Gethsemane.

Help us, God, on the days when everything goes wrong. May we learn to trust you and put our hopes in you, the same as Jesus did. In his name. Amen

19

What Good Is Just One Brick?

"What man of you, having a hundred sheep, if he has lost one of them, does not leave the ninety-nine in the wilderness, and go after the one which is lost, until he finds it?" (Luke 15:4).

Objects: one red brick, one piece from a jigsaw puzzle, one page from a story book.

One brick doesn't seem good for much, does it? But when you see a brick missing from a fireplace it may spoil the looks of that fireplace.

One piece out of a jigsaw puzzle that has five hundred pieces doesn't seem really important. But its absence can spoil the whole picture.

One page torn from a story book can spoil all your reading fun.

One brick, one piece of a jigsaw puzzle, one page torn from a story book—these can be highly important.

So is one person.

Jesus believed that just one person is important.

Once he told a story about a shepherd who had one hundred sheep. The shepherd paid careful attention to each one of them.

Perhaps he knew them all by name. One evening he stood on a little rise in the ground so he could see them all. He counted them. His heart almost failed him. Instead of one hundred sheep he counted only ninety-nine. Right away he began to search for that one sheep. He just *had* to find it.

And find it he did. He picked up the sheep, put it on his shoulder, and came back to his other sheep. He was so glad he found it that he invited all his neighbors to a celebration. It was a wonderful party with laughter and excitement and lots to eat, and all because the shepherd had found one lost sheep.

If one sheep is so important to a shepherd just think how important you and I must be to God!

That is what Jesus is saying in the lost sheep story.

God loves each one of us; every person in the world counts with him.

When one brick is gone from a fireplace that fireplace is incomplete. When one piece is missing from a jigsaw puzzle the picture is ruined. When one page is torn from a book the story can be a failure.

Every one of us is within the reach of God's love. We are so important to him that when we are lost he will search and search for us until he finds us.

O God, we are thankful for Jesus' story of the sheep that got lost and was finally found. We are so glad to know that if we should ever wander away from you we will always be in your care. In the name of Jesus. Amen

20

From a Tiny Seed
to a Good-Sized Tree

" ... the kingdom of heaven is like a grain of mustard seed which a man took and sowed in his field; it is the smallest of all seeds, but when it is grown it is the greatest of shrubs and becomes a tree ... " (Matt. 13:31–32).

Objects: several brightly colored packages containing flower or vegetable seeds. A garden rake or hoe. One package may be opened and a few seeds poured into a child's hand.

Sometime in your life you'll probably want to plant a garden. It is exciting to watch flowers and vegetables grow. Maybe you will live in a city where you will have only a tiny space for a garden or perhaps you'll live where there are large farms. There you will have many acres of land on which to plant your garden.

Suppose you decide to have a flower garden. What kind of seeds will you plant? Here are some packages of seeds: petunias, marigolds, poppies, and castor beans. Maybe you will have some favorite flower that you'll want to see growing in your garden.

You will find that some big plants come from little seeds. See

45

this sunflower seed. It's the kind we like to feed to birds. The seed isn't very large but the plant that grows from it can rise ten or fifteen feet.

Once Jesus told some of his friends about a mustard seed. He said it was the smallest of all seeds, so small that they would find it hard to see one by itself. Yet when it is sowed in a field it grows into a shrub that is as large as a tree. In fact, said Jesus, the shrub grows so large that birds make their nests in its branches.

Jesus told the story of the mustard seed to encourage his .disciples. He wanted them to understand that although the kingdom of heaven had started small they were not to become down-hearted. He promised that like a tiny mustard seed it would grow and grow. Some day it would fill the whole earth.

What is true about the growth of God's kingdom is also true about the growth of God's people.

When you compare yourself with some of your friends you may feel that you don't have much skill at anything. Maybe you say, "I can't draw life-like pictures or sing songs anyone will listen to. I'm really not good at math or spelling. On the playground I'm no great athlete."

Well, if you're about ready to quit, don't. Remember the sunflower and the mustard shrub. They come from small seeds. If you have only a tiny talent it can grow and grow until it becomes really useful to God.

O God, bless any small talents we have. With your help may they grow until they become useful to you. Amen

21

If Disappointment Comes, Don't Quit

"And when they had come opposite Mysia, they attempted to go into Bithynia, but the Spirit of Jesus did not allow them" (Acts 16:7).

Object: a large paper bag containing a pound of coffee, either in a can or in a package.

Even if you don't ever drink coffee I'm sure you see plenty of it around your kitchen. Probably you smell it perking in the morning before you set out for school. Most older people drink it even if it is dreadfully expensive. When you are much older and work at a job you will get to know something called "the coffee break."

A few years ago in California a man's lunch wagon got stuck on a railway track. A train thundered down on the wagon before he could drive it off the crossing. He jumped to safety just in time to see the engine plow into the wagon smashing it to pieces. Just one thing was not destroyed: the man's coffee-maker. While the passengers and spectators stood around staring at the wreck the owner of the wagon got his coffee machine going and sold hot cups of coffee to the bystanders.

Pretty smart! He made the most of a bad business. When all went wrong he saved something from the ruin.

How do you and I handle *our* big troubles? When one of our plans crumbles do we map out another plan and go to work on it?

The first Christians often had to change *their* plans. Again and again they turned their disappointments into opportunities. Once the apostle Paul and some Christian friends intended to go to a city called Bithynia. They were missionaries and wished to tell the story of Jesus to the people of that region. But their way was blocked. They were disappointed but they would not quit telling about Jesus. Although they could not go to Bithynia they went to Macedonia instead. Their first plan was upset; they made the most of another.

How do *you* deal with disappointment? When you have a plan that gets smashed can you work out something else?

Perhaps you had a plan to bring one of your friends to church or to church school to hear about Jesus. So you asked him to come and he promised he would. But he did not keep his promise. So your project did not work. Why not ask another friend?

Maybe you set out to read all the stories in the New Testament about Jesus. But you found some of the words a little too big. So you were disappointed. Try another way of learning about Jesus; why don't you ask your mother and father to read Bible stories to you?

When we try to do a good thing, God, and the way gets blocked, help us to try something else just as good. In Jesus' name. Amen

22

A Potato Is a Potato Is a Potato

"But he who received the one talent, went and dug in the ground and hid his master's money" (Matt. 25:18).

Objects: a small table or stand on which are eight potatoes of about the same size. Five of the potatoes are together on a corner of the table, two are in another corner and one is in a third corner.

Many of us think that we don't have any abilities. We see other girls and boys who are skillful in science, others who can draw clever pictures, still others who are good softball players; yet we are poor in science class, cannot draw pictures that anyone can even understand, and cannot throw a ball from first to second base.

So we feel we can't do much of anything.

We envy all the talents others have, forgetting that we surely do have some skill that is useful and worth putting to work.

Skill or talent is the ability to do a thing well. If we have only one talent still that *is* a talent. What we must do is use that one talent. Five potatoes are better than two potatoes and, of course, much better than one. But that one potato is useful—ask any girl or boy who hasn't eaten anything for a whole day.

Jesus once told a story about a man who had five talents and another who had just two. A third man had only one talent. (The word *talent* as Jesus used it meant a sum of money. But we might think of talents in a different way: as skills or abilities.)

The five-talented man in Jesus' story put his talents to good use and gained five more. The man with two did the same and doubled his talents. But the man with one thought so little of his that he dug a hole in the ground and buried it.

That was a big mistake. He should have put it to work.

In our class in church school we may not be able to answer all the questions the teacher asks. One of your friends in the class always seems to know just the right answers. He waves his hand in the air every single time the teacher asks a question. After awhile maybe you begin to feel depressed. "Aw," you may say to yourself, "I'm really pretty dumb, I don't know much of anything." Well, keep your ears open and your mind alert. A question may come along you can answer satisfactorily.

Your willingness to listen closely is a talent in itself. Don't dig a hole and bury your talent. One talent, one potato, can be very useful.

Father, show us where our abilities are, then help us to use them in your service. In Jesus' name. Amen

23

How Much Can You Give?

"And he saw a poor widow put in two copper coins. And he said, 'Truly I tell you, this poor widow has put in more than all of them' " (Luke 21:2, 3).

Objects: a five dollar bill, a quarter, a dime, a nickel, and a penny. An alternative: a dime bank or piggy bank, containing coins that rattle.

Once a minister, during the offering in a church service, left the pulpit and followed the ushers around as they passed the plates. He looked at every five dollar bill, every quarter, dime, nickel, and penny that members of the congregation gave to the church.

The people were angry; at least many were. They felt the pastor was a spy; they did not want him watching the amount of money they put on the offering plate. They said among themselves, "It's none of his business what we give to God."

When the minister returned to the pulpit he said, "If you are troubled by my watching every penny you put in the offering perhaps you have a right to be. Remember, *God* sees and he has a right to look."

Yes, God does see what we give to his work. And if we give

51

all we ought to give he is pleased with our contribution. He does not expect us to give what we do not have, but he does require us to give gladly and generously.

One day long ago Jesus sat in a room in the Jerusalem temple where people were making their offerings to God. As they gave their money they said out loud just how much they were giving.

Along came a rich man who almost shouted how much he was giving. Other people also made generous gifts. Then a poor woman entered the room and gave all she had to God: two copper coins worth less than one of our pennies. Perhaps she glanced around a little, almost whispering the amount of her gift, hoping no one would hear her when she declared the tiny offering she was making.

But Jesus, when he heard the size of the amount, made a startling remark. He said she put in *more* than all the rich people who seemed so generous.

What did he mean? I'm sure you can guess. He meant that her gift was largest of all because she gave all she had.

If we can make only a small gift to God let us not be ashamed, but make the gift to him gladly and thankfully.

O God, our Father, we confess, because we are selfish, that some-times we have been stingy with you. In the future may all our gifts be pleasing to you. In the name of Jesus. Amen

24

Be Sure to See the Best

"Let love be genuine; hate what is evil, hold fast to what is good" (Rom. 12:9).

Object: a full-size page from a newspaper with a section conspicuously cut out.

What do you see as I hold up this page from a newspaper? A hole in the paper? Something missing?

Why do you suppose we see the hole in the newspaper rather than the pictures, the stories, the advertisements, and the many headlines?

A lot of us seem to be made that way. Sometimes we use expressions like "the fly in the ointment" and "the hair in the biscuit." These sayings mean that even when everything else seems to be just fine, still the first thing that catches our eyes is a flaw, a mistake, or a blunder.

The stories in newspapers are all there for us to read but right away many of us find fault that just one story is missing.

A wise man once said, "hold fast to what is good." Sometimes we hold fast to what is bad. We keep remembering something about a friend that annoys us. In almost every way our teacher at school is helpful to us and kind, but if that teacher has some failing we may remember that and forget her goodness. We are holding fast to that which is unpleasant.

Last week we had several happy days at school. One day was especially good: the art lesson was almost like a game, the music lesson was interesting too, and on the playground at recess we had real fun. But is the thing we remember most the push a boy gave us at the drinking fountain?

Jesus spent his days on earth doing wonderful things for everybody. He healed people who were ill with leprosy—one of the most frightful diseases a human being can suffer from. He made the lame to walk and the blind to see. He even cast demons out of people. His teachings were helpful to all who would listen. He told fascinating stories, the best ever told.

But enemies lay in wait, hoping to catch him in some mistake. They were fault-finders hoping to discover something wrong with him. They could not see what a wonderful person he was, or they did not want to see because they were jealous of him.

The rest of this day and all through the week let us look for the best in our family and friends and teachers. Let us see their kind acts and listen to their kind words. These are the things we should remember. Then we will be holding fast to that which is good.

Our Father, open our eyes to what is good and beautiful all about us. Give us good memories for all the fine things that happen to us. In Jesus' name. Amen

25

Look at the Other Side

"Do not judge by appearances, but judge with right judgment" (John 7:24).

Object: a large rubber ball—half of which is colored red, the other half blue. A round balloon may be substituted for a ball. At the beginning of the presentation the ball may be held up in such a way that the children will see only the blue surface.

What color is this ball? Yes, what you see of the ball is blue. But from where I am it is red. If you make up your mind that you are right about the ball being blue and I say firmly that it is red we can't get anywhere at all.

When I turn the ball around you can see that it is both blue and red.

Things are not always what they seem to be, because we see only a part of them. Perhaps we make up our minds that one of our schoolmates is hard to get along with. He seems kind of cross and bad-tempered. But maybe he just seems that way because you don't know him well. There's another side of him you ought to see—the friendly side.

Perhaps a girl we know at school looks unhappy almost every day. So we have made up our minds that she is sulky and grumpy and mad all the time. Perhaps she only seems that way. Maybe we are seeing only one side of her. It could be there are times when she is pleasant and full of fun.

We think of a certain boy in our grade as being very selfish. We notice that he seems to grab all the good things without thinking of what others may want. But we may be seeing only one side of him. Perhaps at times he is generous and thoughtful of others.

People often took a one-sided view of Jesus. One day he was accused of breaking the law by those who did not like him and would not honestly try to understand his words and acts. They said he was a bad man and that he ought to be punished, that he should even be killed. Blindly they made up their minds about him; they did not judge him by right judgment.

Often, like them, *we* fail to make right judgments. Sometimes we get one-sided ideas about people. We see only a few things about them that annoy us and we decide right away that such people are not worth knowing.

From now on let us try to see another side to all the people we dislike. Perhaps our dislike is narrow minded. If that is true let us begin to judge others with right judgment.

Help us, God, to be fair when we think of others. Keep us from seeing only one side of them. May we judge them as we ourselves want to be judged. Amen

26

A Corner for Silence

" . . . in quietness and in trust shall be your strength . . . "
(Isa. 30:15).

Object: a kitchen rocking chair that can be placed in front of
the children. Either the storyteller or one of the children might
sit in it during the presentation.

Long ago a certain ruler of a far country called for his son who
was some day to become king himself. The ruler said to the boy:
"Once a day for half an hour go into a room by yourself and sit
in quietness. Do not read a book or listen to music. Just sit in
silence."

The boy did as his father requested. Every day for thirty minutes he went alone to a room in the palace and sat in a chair in
silence. Years later he told friends that the half hours spent
alone were the best in his life.

A whole half hour just sitting alone is too much for most of us.
But what about doing that for five minutes every day? Try sitting
in a rocking chair, or any kind of a chair, alone sometime during
the day. This could be a kind of adventure in being still, with no
newspaper, no comic book, no picture magazine, and no TV.

Do you remember hearing about how Jesus would withdraw

from the crowds that followed him? They wanted to hear his teachings or to be healed by the touch of his kindly hands. They ran after him wherever he went: in the cities as well as along the country roads. They never seemed to leave him alone.

But every once in a while he would go away by himself. Sometimes he stayed alone all night in the peacefulness of a mountainside. He did not heal or teach people then. He spent the time in quietness with God.

Perhaps all of us are too noisy. We want to be doing something all the time. And many of the things we do aren't worth very much. We rush about the house inside and out; we turn on the stereo or chem gum in front of the TV. Of course many of our activities are good. But often we are so frisky and loud that we cannot hear God's voice. He would have to shout to be heard above all the racket we are making.

So why not experiment by being alone and still for a few minutes each day? If we cannot have a room by ourselves in our home perhaps we may find just a corner where we may listen to God's voice. Jesus drew great strength from the time he spent alone. It was during these hours by himself that he heard God speak to him, giving him guidance and help.

O God, help us to be quiet a little each day so we can hear you. In the name of Jesus. Amen

27

Some Things to Throw Away

"Let all bitterness and wrath and anger and clamor and slander be put away from you, with all malice, and be kind to one another, tenderhearted, forgiving one another, as God in Christ forgave you" (Eph. 4:31, 32).

Objects: a long rusty spike or nail, badly bent; a battered broom; a broken pane of glass; a large tin can cover with jagged edges; a broken bottle. The objects may be placed on a small stand or table where the children may see them easily.

What do you think of all these things on the table? One by one I'll pick them up so you can see them better. You can tell me as I hold them up what they are. Probably all of you can think of broken or worn-out things you see lying around your home. We call such things rubbish.

Trash and rubbish take up a lot of space. Some of these objects are even dangerous to keep in our houses. For instance, this rusty nail, broken pane of glass, and tin cover could give you painful cuts if you should make a mistake in handling them.

After the service today I'm going to take all these things to our rubbish barrel and throw them away.

Many of the useless and dangerous articles that collect around our homes are clutter, and clutter should be cleaned up and thrown away.

In the New Testament is a verse that tells us what to do with dangerous junk and clutter. If the writer of that verse were standing here beside me he would look at these pieces of trash and say, "Throw out all this trash; toss it on the rubbish pile." But he writes about a different kind of rubbish that we should do away with. He tells us to get rid of rubbish such as anger, spitefulness, grudges, and bad feelings about other people.

Just think of all the rubbish and clutter we carry with us. Some of us dislike a certain schoolmate. There is nothing really bad about him at all, so that dislike of ours is so much rubbish. Why not throw it out right now? Perhaps we have a bad habit of saying unkind, even cruel, words to others. Toss the habit overboard. Some of us are selfish with our belongings; we don't like to share our books and toys with anyone. This selfish spirit is the kind of trash we should get rid of at once.

If we are clinging to anger, spitefulness, grudges, and bad feelings of any kind it is time we dropped these things in some rubbish barrel. But be sure to never throw away a kind and loving spirit.

In our daily living, God, help us to throw away what is bad and harmful and keep what is good and useful. In the name of Jesus. Amen

28

When the Alarm Goes Off, Listen

"Pray for us, for we are sure that we have a clear con-science, desiring to act honorably in all things" (Heb. 13:18).

Object: an alarm clock, fairly large, not electric. Sometime during the presentation the alarm may be set off.

I suppose all of you have alarm clocks at home. Perhaps sometimes your dad sets the alarm for five o'clock in the morning so he will get up to go fishing, or for about seven o'clock to help him get up for work.

Maybe you set the alarm yourself when you need to get up for school or when you want to be on time for a Saturday picnic.

Have you happened to think that there is a kind of alarm clock inside us? Sometimes when it rings we don't pay any attention; we just let it go off and make all the noise it wants to. Maybe we say, "Oh, let the old thing ring, I don't want to be bothered by it."

Perhaps mother has baked brownies that we especially like. She has baked them for friends she is entertaining in the afternoon. Mother offers us just one, telling us that the rest are for company and we must not eat any more. Then she leaves the kitchen for a few minutes. Those brownies sure look good, so good! We're alone in the kitchen, mother can't see us, so we reach out our hand to take one. Suddenly an alarm goes off inside us and reminds us, "Mother said you are not to take any more." Are we going to pay attention to that alarm?

The man who wrote the Book of Hebrews in the New Testament must have had an alarm clock inside him. He was worried that some of his friends were a little suspicious of him. He feared they might not trust him to do the right things. This bothered him so much that he went out of his way to tell those friends that he *was* honest and that he wanted always to act honorably in every way. Then he assured them that he had a clear conscience. This man listened when the alarm rang.

Once in a while we are asked to do things we know we should not do. Other times we fail to do the things we ought to do. Maybe we are tempted to tell a lie or to speak angry words to a schoolmate or to take for our own something that belongs to somebody else. Then perhaps our conscience will give us a signal and we will hear an alarm go off inside us. Let us be sure to listen carefully and obey the signal.

Like the writer of the Book of Hebrews we will want to have a clear conscience.

O God, help us every day to listen to your voice as you speak to us in our hearts. We truly want to obey your will and be the kind of people you want us to be. In the name of Jesus. Amen

29

What's That on Your Back?

"Come to me, all who labor and are heavy-laden, and I will give you rest" (Matt. 11:28).

Object: a knapsack of any kind that will fit a child's back. One of the children might be asked to put on the knapsack which should contain weights of some kind.

Perhaps during the summer you went hiking with your parents and your father carried a back pack something like this. Maybe you carried a smaller one on your back that contained a thermos bottle, a sandwich, and about four chocolate cookies.

After you had hiked a long way the pack seemed really heavy. You were sure it got heavier each mile you walked. Finally you decided to take it off, take out some of the cookies and rest awhile.

Many of us carry packs on our backs that cannot be seen. These invisible packs can become painfully heavy. Some of us carry grudges and those grudges get heavier and heavier the longer we carry them. Others of us carry memories that hurt. They get heavy too. We wish that someone would come along and take such packs off our back.

If we trust him Jesus will do just that. Once he was talking to a large crowd. As he looked at their faces he felt a great pity for the people. His heart went out to them in a wave of kindly feeling. He wanted to heal their diseases and comfort their sorrows. He wanted to take their packs from their shoulders, for he knew many of them were weighed down by worries and illnesses, fears and heartaches. He so badly wanted to help them with their burdens that he cried to them, "Come to me, all who labor and are heavy laden, and I will give you rest."

When we read these words we may feel that Jesus was talking only to adults. And some adults seem to think that girls and boys carry no burdens at all.

I think older people who believe that are wrong. There is really a pack of some kind on just about everybody's back. Some of us carry a burden of loneliness; we want friends but do not know how to win or keep them. Others have a pack of fears on their backs. We are afraid our report cards may show low grades, or we are afraid the teacher doesn't like us. And a few of us are heavily laden with guilt feelings because we know we have let down a brother or sister or friend and we do not like ourselves at all.

To all of us who are lonely or fearful or guilty Jesus gives an invitation. He invites us to come to him. If we walk with him and talk with him he will help us. The better we get to know him the lighter will become the pack on our back.

Thank you, God, for caring for us, for helping us with our troubles, and for being with us all the time. Amen

30

Being Big Isn't Always Important

"Then David said to the Philistine, 'You come to me with a sword and with a spear and with a javelin; but I come to you in the name of the Lord of hosts, the God of the armies of Israel, whom you have defied' " (I Sam. 17:45).

Object: a sling-shot preferably a primitive version; that is, a leather pocket with a stout cord tied to each end. Children will be more interested in this ancient form of the weapon than in the Y-shaped sling that is common now. Either is easy to make.

Do all grown-up people seem big and tall to you? When they are standing all around you after the church service is over do you have to hold your head far back to look up into their faces? Do you feel squeezed and kind of weighed down? Perhaps you think, with all those big people towering above you and talking over your head, that because you're so small you don't count for very much.

Well sometimes little people are more powerful than big people.

Maybe you remember the story of David the Israelite and Goliath the Philistine. The people of Israel were afraid of Goliath because he was nine-and-a-half feet tall and a savage fighter.

His spear tip alone weighed eleven pounds or more. But David was not afraid of Goliath and he determined to do battle with the huge soldier.

David's friends warned him that he would be killed by Goliath, but David was not frightened at all. He got out his sling-shot, picked up a few stones for ammunition, and then went out to face Goliath. You'd have to say that it was a pigmy against a giant.

After some talk back and forth between the two enemies David dropped a stone into his sling and let fly at the gigantic Goliath, hitting him in the forehead. The giant was stunned and fell over; then David rushed up and killed him.

Don't let anyone tell you that Mister Big always wins. He doesn't! Sometimes the little people beat the big people. Because you think you're pretty small don't get the idea that you count for nothing. Almighty God was with David and David knew he had God's support. He was not afraid of anybody, not even of a nine-and-a-half foot giant.

Whether we are big or little, it is great to know that God is our friend and will help us at all times. If we are asked to do something good for our parents, our teacher, our church, we should never think about how little we are, but about how God will be our helper.

Give us strength, O God, to do what you want us to do. Even when we feel small or weak never let us forget that you are great and strong. As you helped David so long ago we pray that you will help us, too. In the name of Jesus. Amen

31

Some Balloons Are for Pricking

"Now the word of the Lord came to Jonah . . ., saying, 'Arise, go to Nineveh, that great city, and cry against it; for their wickedness has come up before me' " (Jonah 1:1, 2).

Object: before story time partially inflate a balloon on which is painted—however roughly—a face of a hobgoblin. During the presentation the balloon may be further inflated, thus enlarging the painted face.

At school during recess time the teacher asked a boy named Pete not to play so roughly in a kickball game. Instead of behaving as the teacher asked, Pete was rude. When his parents heard about what had happened on the playground they told Pete to apologize to the teacher the next day when he went to school. He said he would but then he began to think how hard it is to apologize. He thought perhaps the words he must say to the teacher would stick in his throat. He was afraid, too, that she would punish him in some way. Saying "I'm sorry" was surely hard work.

The more Pete worried about what he must do the bigger his problem got. It became so big he could not go right to sleep the night before. The next day when he *did* say "I'm sorry" the teacher forgave him.

When we worry and fret about some job we must do that job gets bigger and bigger until it seems we just can't do it.

Once a long time ago, God told a man named Jonah to warn the people of a certain city that because of their wickedness their city would be destroyed. Jonah was scared. The more he thought about that job the more he feared what would happen to him when he told the people about their wickedness. His fears grew and grew until he was so frightened that, instead of obeying God and going to the sinful city, he ran away. If only he had trusted God his fears would not have grown so big.

Jonah finally did as God commanded and warned the people who lived in the city. He could have saved himself a lot of trouble if he had trusted God and obeyed him.

When we have jobs to do or problems to solve or worries to overcome we can trust God to help us. To be sure, God won't solve all our problems or perform all our tasks for us, but he will surely stand by us.

When we trust him many of our fears will disappear just as the face on this balloon will vanish when I prick it with a pin.

God our Father, we need your help all the time. There are so many things we cannot do all by ourselves. May our faith in you help us to do what we ought to do without being afraid. In your name we pray. Amen

32

Put Shoes on Your Good Ideas

" . . . a man had two sons; and he went to the first and said, 'Son, go and work in the vineyard today.' And he answered, 'I will not'; but afterward he repented and went. And he went to the second and said the same; and he answered, 'I go, sir,' but he did not go." (Matt. 21:28–30).

Objects: two shoes—not mates. One is obviously new showing no wear. The other shows that the owner has done a great deal of walking; perhaps the heel is worn on one side.

See how different these two shoes are. One is shiny and new, the other worn and old. The old shoe has been worn and worn. It has been put to work just as some of our good ideas should have been put to work.

One windy, rainy morning a certain girl looked out her kitchen window and saw that the newspaper left by the newsboy on old Mrs. Jones's porch had blown off and was lying on the ground. The girl said to herself, "I ought to go over there and put the paper inside her screen door so that it won't blow all over her lawn." But she just *thought* about doing it, ate her breakfast, and did not rescue the newspaper. She had a great idea. All she had to do was put shoes on the idea and cross the street on a kind errand. Instead she forgot all about Mrs. Jones's newspaper.

Before we scold the girl for failing to carry out her kind thought we may think how many of *our* good ideas get the same treatment. Often we do not put shoes on our good ideas.

We meant to thank mother for her good cooking and for the delicious berry pie she baked awhile ago. We meant to thank dad for taking us on a picnic last month. We intended to visit one of the girls in our grade in school who broke her leg when she fell off her bike. We thought of telling the teacher how much we liked the last science lesson.

What good ideas we have! Did we put shoes on them? Did we *do* those things or just think about doing them?

One day Jesus told a story about a father and his two sons. The father asked the first son to go to work in their vineyard. The boy said, "I will not." But when he thought over his father's command he was sorry he said no, so he went to work in the vineyard. The father told the second son to go to work. "I go, sir," said the boy. But he never went.

The second boy had good intentions but he did not carry them out. Often our own ideas and plans are so very good! Let us this week and from now on put shoes on those plans and put them to work.

O God, we want to serve you, and we want to do the good things you expect of us. But sometimes we are lazy, and so we do only what is easy. Every day help us to do your will. In Jesus' name. Amen

33

Don't Forget the Towel

*"If I then, your Lord and Teacher, have washed your feet,
you also ought to wash one another's feet. For I have given
you an example, that you also should do as I have done to you"*
(John 13:14, 15).

Objects: a large towel; a small, gold-colored cross; and a shiny
brass candlestick.

Many churches have a cross on the communion table, or hung
from the wall in front of the congregation. Also in some
churches you will find beautiful candleholders setting on the
table. These are good-looking objects and add to the attractive-
ness of the church.

This towel I am holding isn't beautiful at all. Really it's just a
piece of rough undecorated cloth. You might think that the cross
and the candlestick are worth a lot more money than this
kitchen towel. And in a way you would be right. But think how
useful a towel can be; it can be put to work.

Once after Jesus had eaten supper with his friends he used a
towel in service to them. He took a basin of water and washed
his disciples' feet that were dusty from walking along the road.
Then he dried them with a towel.

Although Jesus was the Savior and Lord of all his friends he became the servant of them all. When he took a towel and dried their feet he showed them just the way they should treat others. They should not try to boss others around, or push them around, but should serve them. He was showing them what to do.

When we are on the playground at school how do we treat other children? Do we try to make everybody do the things we want to do and play the games we like to play? Do we sometimes try to show that we are stronger and smarter than they? Perhaps we go our own way and pay no attention to the needs and wishes of others.

Jesus urges us to care about all the children of the world who are in need (any kind of need), starting right here with our brothers and sisters and schoolmates. Children we go to school with may be lonely and need our friendship. Let us be ready every day to walk and talk and play with them.

When Jesus took a towel and washed his disciples' feet he showed he was glad to help and serve them. He expects us to help and serve all who are in need.

Help us, God, to put away any pride we have and seek to serve others in any way we can. Open our eyes to the hurts of all who are lonely and unhappy. May we learn how to say the words and do the things that will encourage them. In the name of Jesus. Amen

34

Don't Neglect the Corners

"Jesus said to him, 'If you wish to go the whole way, go, sell your possessions and give to the poor, and then you will have riches in heaven; and come, follow me' " (Matt. 19:21, NEB).

Object: a window pane about eight by twelve inches. The glass is clean in the center, but the corners are stained and obviously dirty.

Sometimes as you walk along the streets of a big city you may see a brave fellow far up on the side of the building washing windows. Maybe he is as far up in the air as twenty-five stories, or even higher. You say to yourself, "Wow! I'd hate to be up in the air that high. If that guy should fall it would be the end of him." So maybe you pretend you're in an airplane and you fly up near to him and shout, "Hey, you be careful. Don't fall off the side of that building."

Well, windows need washing. Somebody must do the job. Do you suppose the man on the side of the building washes in all the corners of the window panes? Perhaps he says to himself: "I'm risking my life up here in the air. People can't expect me to be too fussy about this job. I'll just get the center of the glass clean and never mind the corners."

If that is what he does you can guess what would happen to him. Even if he didn't fall off the side of the building he might fall out of a job. Hired to be a kind of fly on a wall he would be expected to do the job right, to go the whole way.

When we become followers of Jesus we are invited to go the whole way with him. He expects us to obey God completely. We can be sure he wants our full obedience because of something that happened as Jesus and his friends were going from city to city helping people.

While Jesus was healing and teaching, a young fellow rushed .up to him and asked how to become one of his followers. He was a fine young man who had been doing many good things. He had always obeyed God's commandments—even when he was a little boy. But he wasn't satisfied with himself; he knew he lacked something. Jesus said to him, "If you wish to go the whole way, sell your possessions and give to the poor, and then you will have riches in heaven."

The young man turned away. He was willing to go only part way with Jesus. There was a corner of his life that needed cleaning. He would do nothing about that corner.

Each one of us is invited by Jesus to go the whole way. This means doing God's will in *all* things, not just most things. It means saying to God, "Not my will, but your will is my guide."

We thank you, God, that you have invited us to walk with you every day. Help us to be willing to go all the way with you, not just part of the way. In Jesus' name. Amen

35

Let's Go Fishing

"There is a lad here who has five barley loaves, and two fish . . . " (John 6:9).

Objects: any kind of fishing rod. Assorted fishing equipment, such as a reel, a line, a tackle box, sinkers, bobbers, hooks.

Maybe some of you like to go fishing. It is a lot of fun. You stand beside a stream or pond and throw out your line and wait. Suddenly you feel a tug on the line, the rod bends, and you pull back in a hurry. All at once there's a splash and you jerk a fish out of the water. You bring the fish home, and your mother cooks it for dinner. You feel mighty proud of yourself for making the catch.

Perhaps the fish you catch won't be a whopper—about so long. But it is big enough to keep and big enough to eat. That fish is good for something.

Here is how Jesus made use of two small fish.

He was on a hillside far from home. It was late in the afternoon. He had been talking to many people who were gathered about him and were listening closely to all he said. They never *thought* of eating until he was through speaking. But when he had finished talking, suddenly they knew they were hungry.

The trouble was they had not brought their lunches and were too far from a store to buy bread and meat.

A boy was there who had been fishing and had caught two small fish. He offered them to Jesus and Jesus used them to feed the hungry people. It was a wonderful thing that Jesus did. It was a generous thing the boy did.

Jesus can use our small contributions. Perhaps we feel that what we have to offer him is so small and unimportant he will never notice our gift. Well, our gifts need not be large or expensive ones if we give them gladly and they are all we can afford.

Surely Jesus did not take the fish away from the boy. He did not say, "Here you, boy, give me those fish; I need them to feed a hungry crowd." When the boy saw Jesus' need for the fish we can imagine he came forward and gave them gladly.

He was glad to help, pleased to be of service. To give our service to Jesus is the greatest thing we can do.

Sometimes when we go fishing we don't get a bite right away. We throw out our line and wait and wait. That's a good time to do some thinking. It's a good time to think of ways we can make a gift to God.

We have no expensive gifts for you, O God. But what we do have we gladly give. In the name of Jesus. Amen

36

Be Sure You're Plugged In

" . . . in all these things we are more than conquerors through him who loved us" (Rom. 8:37).

Object: a long electric extension cord with a light bulb at one end. The cord is not connected to electric power at first but may be plugged in toward the conclusion of the presentation.

We have here a long electric cord with a light bulb at its end. The bulb will not give any light, and of course you see why it won't. It is not connected to the electric current.

Sometimes at home we turn on the TV, but it doesn't come on. We give the dials a turn; still nothing happens. Then we begin an investigation. After awhile we find that the cord which connects the TV to electric power is not plugged in. So we get down on our knees, plug it in, and get a picture.

A certain boy likes to play with his electric train that is in the basement of his home. Perhaps we ought to say that the boy and his dad like to play with their electric train. (Dad has as much fun running the train as his son does.) Almost every day they go downstairs to make it go.

One cloudy day when he could not have much fun outside, the boy went down to the basement to play with the train. He quickly turned on the switch and, you guessed it, nothing happened. The train was not connected to electric power.

Paul, the great missionary who wrote many of the letters in the New Testament, was a man who was linked with a mighty power. He did not have an easy life and endured many kinds of trouble. Sometimes he was beaten by his enemies, often he was laughed at, several times he was thrown into prison, and three times he was shipwrecked. About all the bad things that can happen to anybody happened to him.

Without God's power added to his own strength he never could have endured all his hardships.

Although we may never suffer as he did, still we do have troubles. And we can depend upon help from the same source that gave Paul his strength. God is a power source we can always depend on.

When we are called unpleasant names by a schoolmate, where can we get the power to forgive? When we have done poor work at school in spelling, or art, or social studies, where can we get the strength to do better next time? When we are trying to carry out some task that seems beyond our ability, where may we go for help? In all these things God will be our helper.

We need never depend only on our own strength. We can depend upon the strength of God. When we pray we are linking ourselves to his power.

Once in a while, God, we know we do not have the strength to do the things we ought to do. We have a lot of problems and troubles. You can help us, Lord, for we put our trust in your power. In Jesus' name. Amen

37

What I Found Beside the Road

" . . . consider the lilies of the field, how they grow; they neither toil nor spin; yet I tell you, even Solomon in all his glory was not arrayed like one of these" (Matt. 6:28, 29).

Objects: an empty soft drink bottle, part of a newspaper, a crumpled brown paper bag, a battered paper cup, a torn paper plate, an empty beer can, a small, crushed cardboard box.

Can you guess where I found these things? They were not in our attic or garage or in any of the rooms in our house. They were not found in our back yard nor on our front lawn.

They are things I saw when I was riding along the highway in our car. Almost every time I looked out the car window I saw tin cans, empty bottles, and all kinds of junk.

You and I know how they got there. When people finished using what was in them they threw them out the car window. Nearly every place you drive you will find rubbish beside the road.

Sometimes when you go hiking on a trail in one of our national forests you'll see waste paper, sandwich wrappers, and plastic cups scattered everywhere. I have seen rusty tin cans at the bottom of clear running streams, and lakeside shores sprinkled with lunch bags and discarded boxes.

It is hard to believe that we so carelessly use the beautiful world that God has given us. Think of all the wonderful scenery we can enjoy in our country! Our land is rich in shining rivers, high mountains, grassy lakes, and giant forests. Almost anywhere you drive you can see these pretty gifts that come from God.

One day as Jesus was teaching he spoke of the beauty of flowers. He and his disciples must have been outside walking in a lovely place. He asked his friends to notice some lilies growing in a nearby field. He told them that those lilies were more beautiful than the clothes of any king. Probably you and I have never seen a king, but we surely do know that flowers are beautiful and that we should take good care of the countryside where they grow.

God who made the earth invites us to use it, not abuse it.

Let us make a resolution to keep his world clean. We might say: "I resolve never to litter the roadside, never to toss paper bags out of our car window, nor throw paper cups under our picnic table or candy wrappers on the school ground or sidewalk. I will treat God's world with respect."

O God, thank you for the world you made and for letting us live in it. Keep us from spoiling any of the beautiful things that are here. Instead may we learn to use them wisely. In the name of Jesus. Amen

38

Time to Take Off Your Shoes

" . . . do not come near; put off your shoes from your feet, for the place on which you are standing is holy ground" (Exod. 3:5).

Objects: a collection of several kinds of shoes.

See this collection of shoes: old ones that need polishing, new ones that shine. Here is a big black one, also a brown one, and even one that is white. On the table you'll see a sandal, a sneaker, and a lady's slipper. And here is one shoe that a baby can wear. Some of these shoes are made to work in, others we would want to wear to a party or church supper.

Probably you can think of many other kinds of shoes you have seen. Perhaps you have a pair at home that is different from any that you can see on the table.

If we had no shoes at all we sure would learn a lot about sore feet. But it is sometimes fun to go barefoot. I often wonder whether store managers ever walk around without their shoes. They are forever putting up signs (for a good reason) on the doors and windows of their markets that read No Bare Feet or Bare Feet Not Allowed.

Shoes do protect our feet from nails and broken glass. They

81

help to keep us warm when it's cold. Some mothers and fathers like us to wear them because they want us to look dressed up.

Once thousands of years ago God spoke to a man named Moses and told him, "Put off your shoes." Perhaps you remember the story about him as told in the third chapter of the Book of Exodus in the Old Testament. Moses was a shepherd. All at once while he was tending sheep he saw a bush on fire. Strangely it did not burn up. Moses was puzzled so he went close to look at the flaming bush. Suddenly God spoke to him out of the fiery bush and said, "Put off your shoes from your feet, for the place on which you are standing is holy ground."

We may live all our lives and never hear God speaking to us just like that. But each time we come to worship in the church we are on holy ground.

When the Bible is read then God is speaking to us, and we can know that we are in a holy place. God does not say to us when we come to worship him, "Take off your shoes," but something inside us may speak up and say, "Be still, be quiet, listen, you are now in a holy place."

Of course all God's world is holy ground. He made the world and all things in it. So whether we are inside the church or outside it we should be ready to listen when he speaks to us.

Show us, O God, how to bow our hearts as well as our heads when you speak to us. May we always listen with reverence and respect to your voice. Amen

39

What Christmas Is All About
(Christmas)

"For to you is born this day in the city of David a Savior, who is Christ the Lord. And this will be a sign for you: you will find a babe wrapped in swaddling clothes and lying in a manger" (Luke 2:11, 12).

Objects: a large paper bag containing a red candle, a length of tinsel, three feet of red ribbon, a large Christmas card, a bright Christmas tree ornament. During the presentation articles may be taken from the paper bag, displayed, and placed on a table or small stand.

I'm glad Christmas time has come again. Probably you are too. Think of the good time we'll have on Christmas: we'll have fun opening our own presents and watching others open theirs. We'll eat a big dinner. The day will seem different in many ways from every other day in the year.

Perhaps you'll see some things around your home that you see only in December. Here is a red ribbon. You may know that your mother uses red ribbon once in awhile during the year, but at Christmas it's all over the place. And here is a sparkling star that can decorate the top of a Christmas tree. (I wish this bag had been big enough to include a green fir tree.) Here is a red candle, a candy cane, and some shiny tinsel. At Christmas we'll see all these things and many more.

Besides enjoying Christmas dinner, our tree, and the gifts we give and get we'll remember on this day that we celebrate the birth of Jesus our Savior and King.

Most of us will celebrate Christmas in a warm and comfortable room. It was very different when Mary gave birth to her son Jesus. He was born in a barn. We make his birth in a stable sound pretty and pleasant, but have you ever thought how cold and miserable a stable can be? Jesus' mother was in pain, Joseph his father was worried, and the baby when he was born must have been uncomfortable. Hay in a barn is fun to jump in, and toss around, but it isn't the best kind of mattress. When you try to sleep on it dust gets in your nose and straws stick in your ears.

Well, Jesus was born in a stable and put in a manger filled with hay. You might think that a barn is hardly a fit birthplace for our Savior and King. And you would be right. But no matter where it took place, Jesus' birth was the greatest thing that ever happened on this earth.

I hope the Christmas lights, red ribbon, and all the pretty gifts will not make you forget the birthday of Jesus.

O God, we don't want to forget that on Christmas we celebrate the birthday of your son. Not only do we want to remember him during that day but on all the days of the year. In his name. Amen